Usborne Quicklinks

For links to websites where you can watch video clips of all kinds of trains, go to the Usborne Quicklinks website at **www.usborne.com/quicklinks** and type in the title of this book. Please follow the internet safety guidelines at the Usborne Quicklinks website.

The Usborne

BIG BOOK
OF TRAINS

Written by Megan Cullis

Illustrated by Gabriele Antonini
Designed by Stephen Wright

Train expert: Anthony Coulls, The National Railway Museum

Pulling power

Early trains were powered by a type of engine called a steam locomotive. The steam locomotive pulled lots of heavy wagons behind it.

The blue part of the train is the locomotive.

This American steam locomotive was called a **Union Pacific Big Boy**.

Steam locomotives pulled a wagon called a tender. It contained coal, which powered the engine.

The Big Boy had the power to pull 100 loaded wagons.

This Big Boy was built to run at 80km/h (50m/h). It dragged heavy wagons across the mountains of Wyoming and Utah.

The **QJ locomotive** is almost twice as heavy as many modern passenger locomotives.

Chimney, where steam and smoke came out

The **Green Arrow** was so powerful it could pull over twenty coaches full of passengers.

Coal was burned inside this firebox. The fire heated up water in the boiler to produce steam.

The steam powered the engine, which turned the wheels around.

Boiler

These rods moved together so the wheels turned around at the same time.

Steam giants

Here are some of the biggest steam locomotives ever built. They were all made over fifty years ago, and many are now out of service.

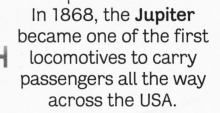

This **LNWR 'jumbo'** locomotive pulled an express passenger train which ran from England to Scotland until 1934.

In 1868, the **Jupiter** became one of the first locomotives to carry passengers all the way across the USA.

This **Yellowstone** locomotive hauled massive loads of iron ore from quarries and factories in Minnesota, USA.

This streamlined **3801** used to carry passengers across Australia.

This **QJ** locomotive transported coal from mines in Inner Mongolia, China. Some are still being used today.

Built in 1936, the **Green Arrow** was designed to carry passengers and heavy goods from London, England to Glasgow, Scotland.

The **Southern Pacific 4449** is a Californian passenger train, which still runs today.

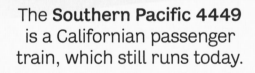

This **Garratt** locomotive hauled coal up steep tracks in South Africa.

This American **Milwaukee Road class A** was an express passenger train, which went from Chicago, Illinois to Saint Paul, Minnesota. It ran between 1935 and 1949.

Dual headlights

The Jupiter's enormous chimney was called a balloon stack. It contained a special mesh to stop sparks from escaping.

This was called a cowcatcher, because it pushed stray cattle off the tracks.

The **Southern Pacific 4449** can travel at speeds of 180km/h (110mph) – the same speed as many modern locomotives.

The **Jupiter** ran on wood rather than coal.

Cab, where the driver sat

JUPITER

JUPITER

Faster and faster

By the 1930s, steam locomotives were being designed to pull faster trains over long distances, without stopping at stations in between.

Mallard was the fastest steam locomotive ever built. It set a world record of 202km/h (126mph) in 1938.

This is the **Flying Scotsman**. Built in 1923, it was the first train that ran non-stop from London to Edinburgh.

This superheater tube made the steam hotter and the engine more powerful.

Chimney

Steam flowed up these pipes and out through the chimney.

Its smooth, curved front helped it to cut through the air.

N4468

This was called a dynamometer car – a special coach containing instruments to measure the locomotive's speed and power.

The locomotive's wheels were hidden behind heavy metal plates, which gave the train its smooth, sleek appearance.

Mountain trains

High up in the mountains, some trains climb up steep slopes, while others travel along long, winding tracks.

The **Darjeeling Toy Train** (called 'toy' because it is so small) weaves through the Himalayan mountains in India. It rises about 2,000m (6,560ft) – that's about 350 storeys high.

It's not powerful enough to climb up steep slopes, so the train makes long, looping zigzags up the mountains.

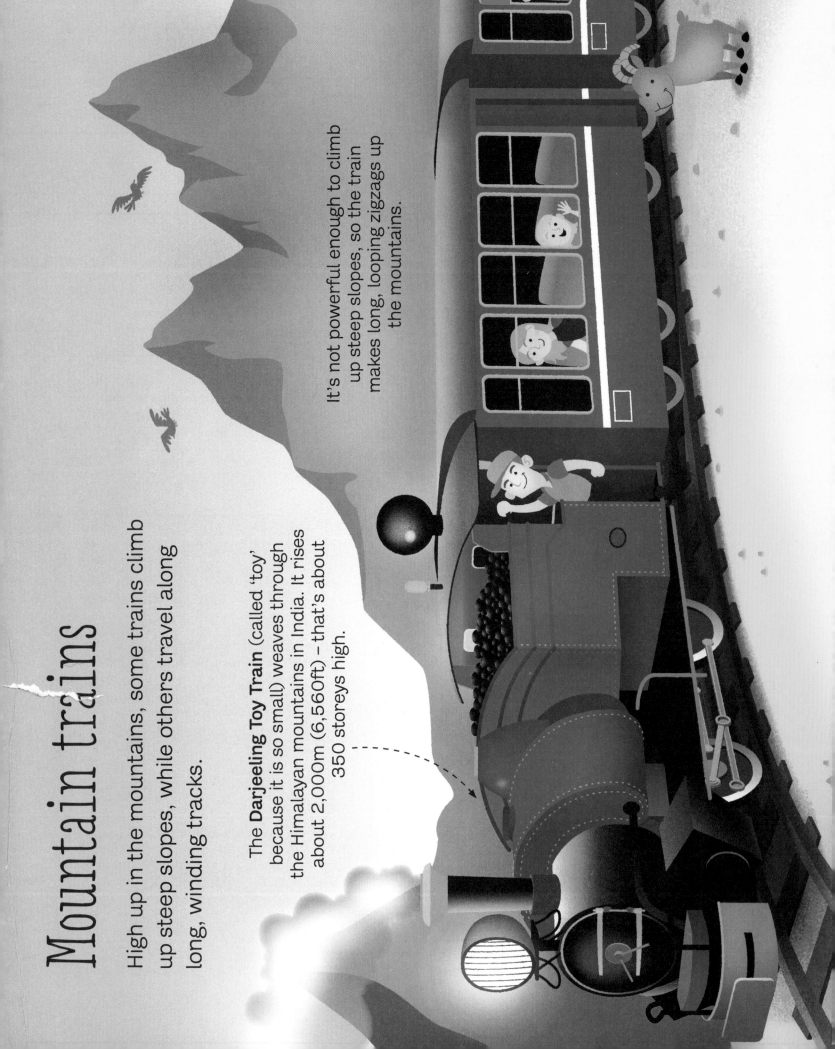

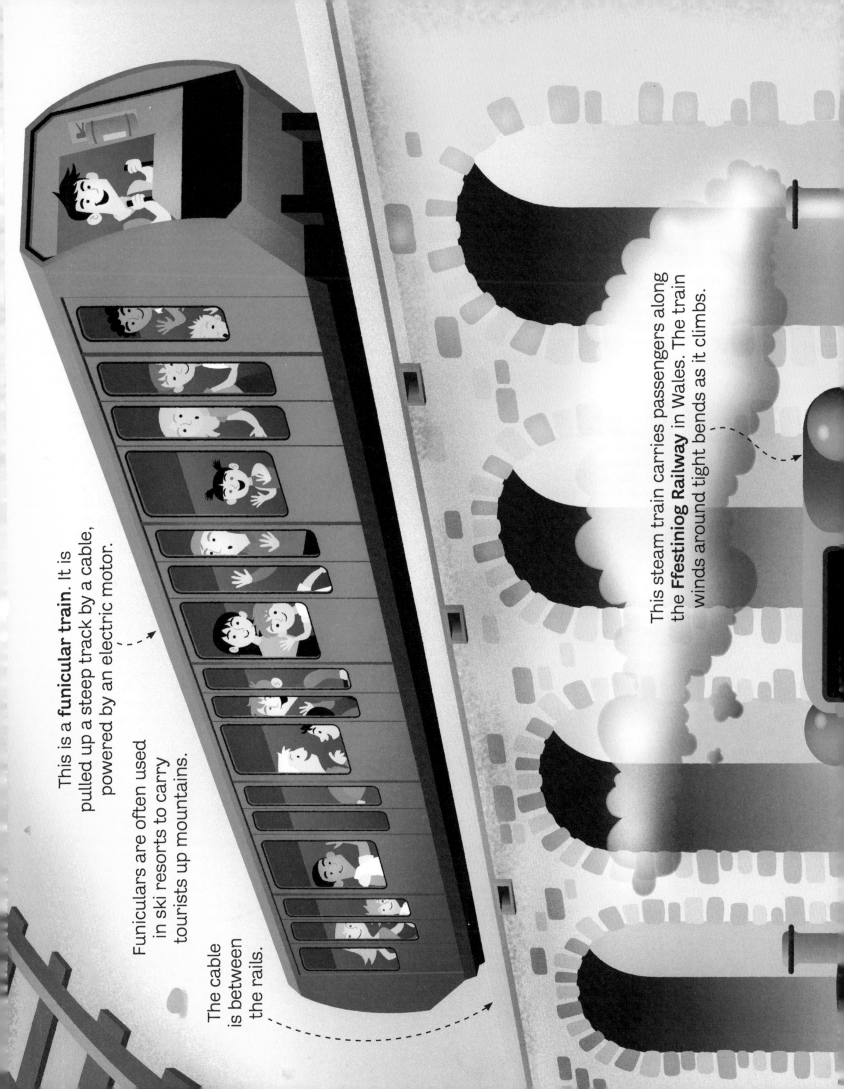

This is a **funicular train**. It is pulled up a steep track by a cable, powered by an electric motor.

Funiculars are often used in ski resorts to carry tourists up mountains.

The cable is between the rails.

This steam train carries passengers along the **Ffestiniog Railway** in Wales. The train winds around tight bends as it climbs.

FLYING SCOTSMAN

Boiler- - - - - -

Firebox - - -

A stoker shovelled
coal into the firebox.

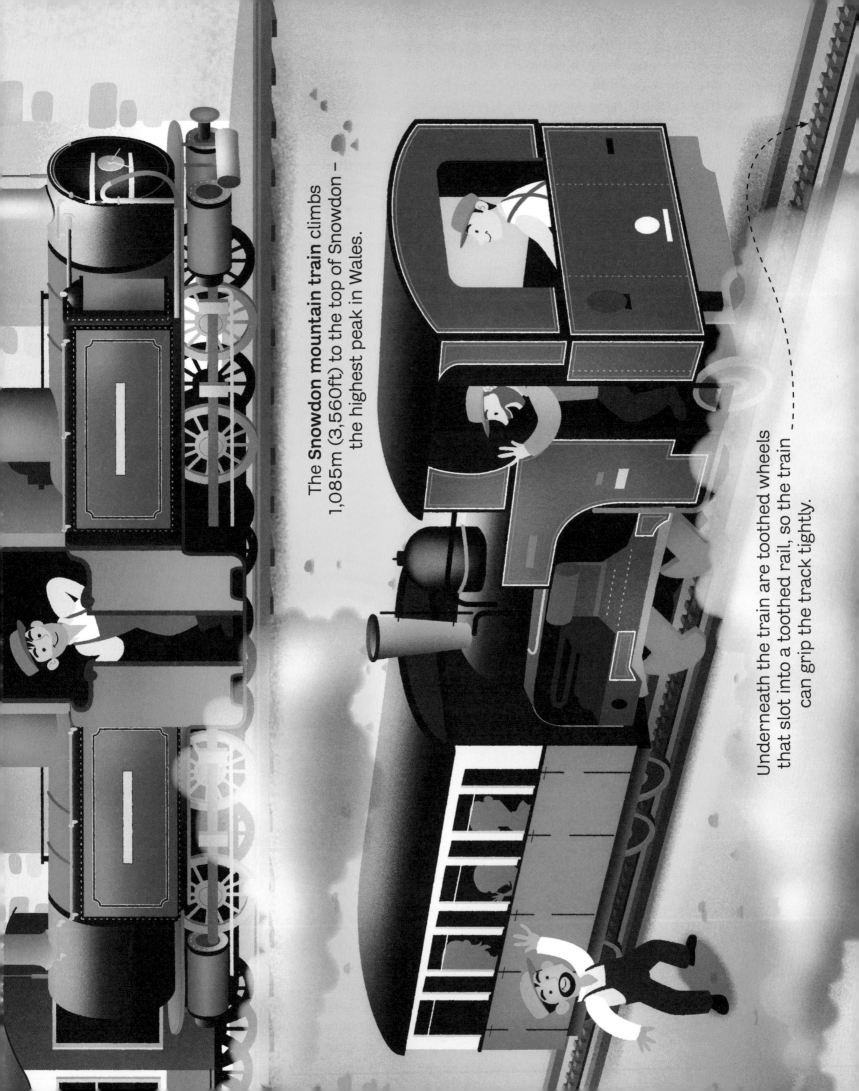

The **Snowdon mountain train** climbs 1,085m (3,560ft) to the top of Snowdon – the highest peak in Wales.

Underneath the train are toothed wheels that slot into a toothed rail, so the train can grip the track tightly.

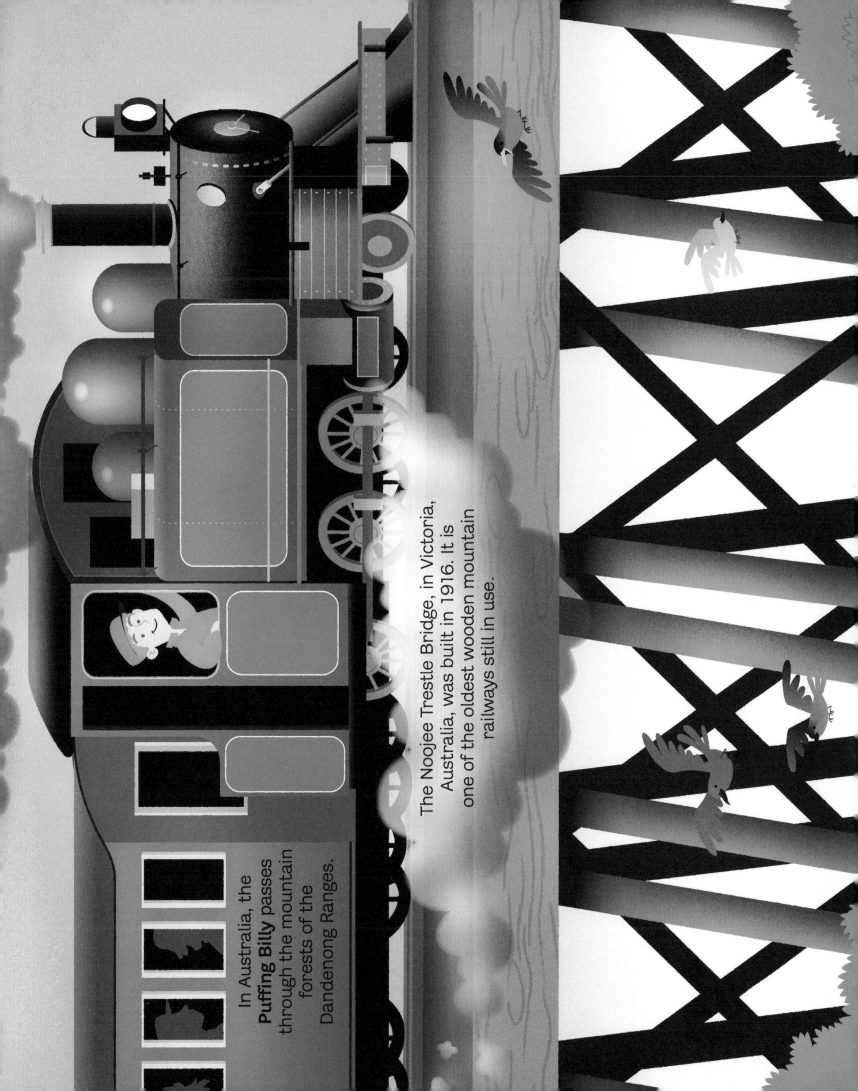

In Australia, the **Puffing Billy** passes through the mountain forests of the Dandenong Ranges.

The Noojee Trestle Bridge, in Victoria, Australia, was built in 1916. It is one of the oldest wooden mountain railways still in use.

Diesel trains

From the 1930s onwards, locomotives that ran on diesel fuel began to replace steam locomotives.

This **Deltic** carried passengers at speeds of up to 161km/h (100mph).

There were cabs both at the front and the back of this locomotive. This way the train could be driven in both directions without having to turn around.

The **Santa Fe F7** had a huge, curved front, which became known as a 'bulldog nose'.

It pulled the **Super Chief** – a luxury passenger train that ran from Kansas City to Los Angeles, USA, between 1936 and 1971.

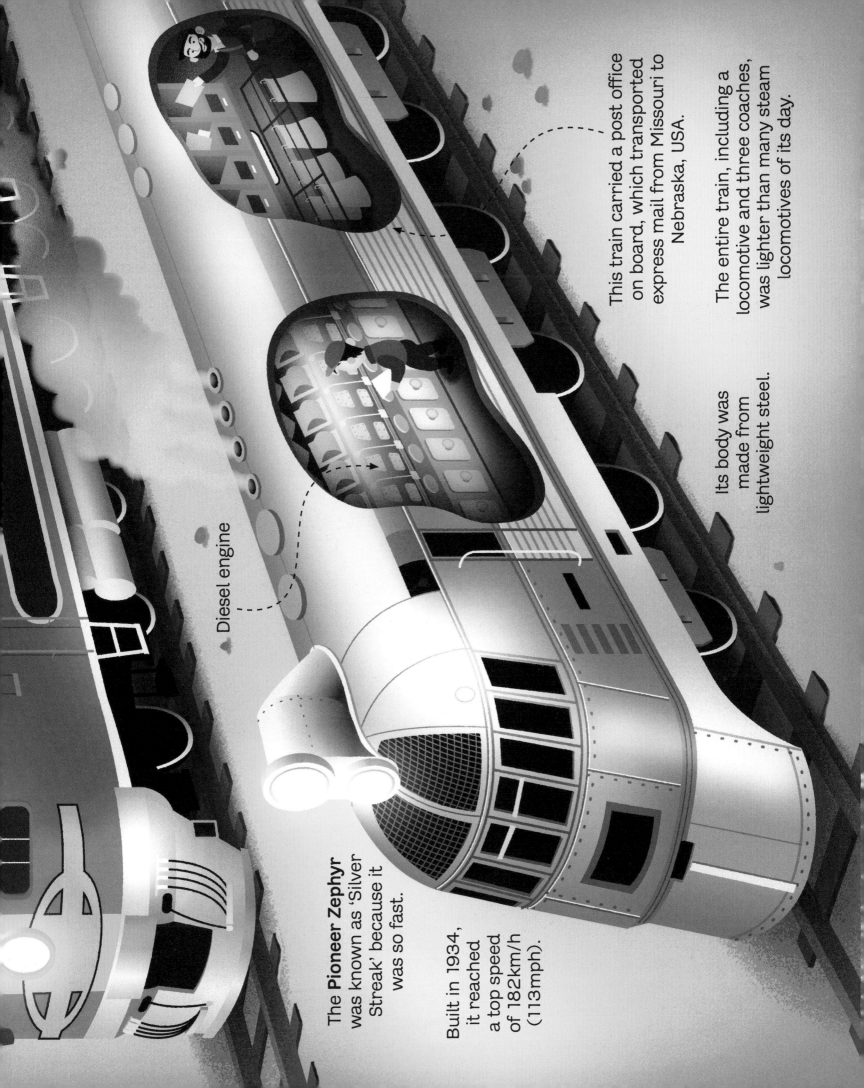

Diesel engine

The **Pioneer Zephyr** was known as 'Silver Streak' because it was so fast.

Built in 1934, it reached a top speed of 182km/h (113mph).

This train carried a post office on board, which transported express mail from Missouri to Nebraska, USA.

The entire train, including a locomotive and three coaches, was lighter than many steam locomotives of its day.

Its body was made from lightweight steel.

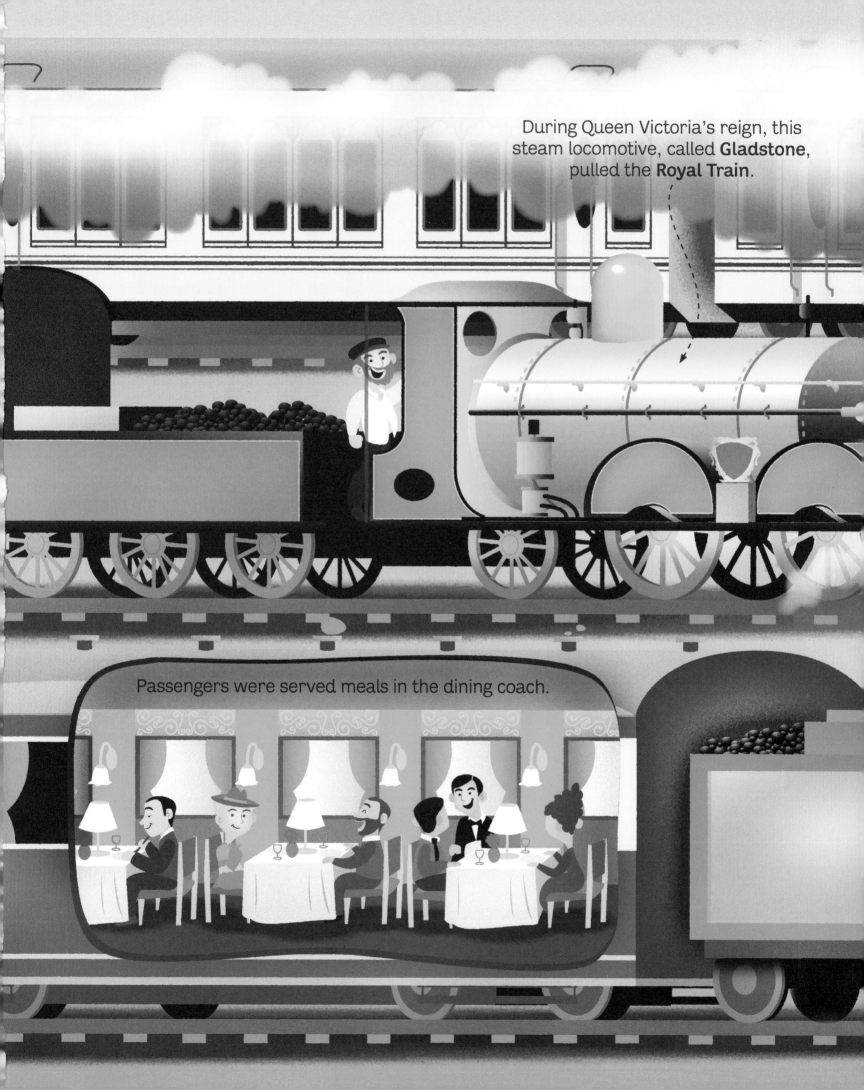

During Queen Victoria's reign, this steam locomotive, called **Gladstone**, pulled the **Royal Train**.

Passengers were served meals in the dining coach.

Inside the Queen's private coach, the rooms were furnished in polished maple and expensive silk.

Reading room

Luxury trains

Some railway companies offer luxury journeys, where passengers can travel in comfort and style.

The **Orient Express** went between Paris in France and Istanbul in Turkey. It ran from 1870, for over 100 years.

The luxurious **Ghan** takes two whole days to travel from the top of Australia to the bottom, stopping at Alice Springs on the way.

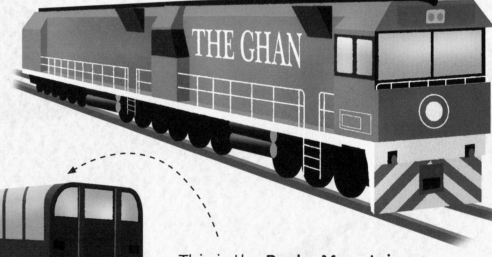

This is the **Rocky Mountaineer**, which winds through the Canadian Rockies. Passengers can admire the views from a luxury glass domed coach.

The **Fairy Queen** is the oldest steam train still running today. It takes passengers from Delhi to Alwar in India.

The **Pride of Africa** takes passengers from South Africa to Namibia and Tanzania.

The glamorous **Royal Canadian Pacific** train is pulled by a diesel locomotive from the 1930s.

The **Palace on Wheels** is an Indian luxury tourist train. It takes eight days to travel from New Delhi to Agra, in Rajasthan.

The **Royal Train** was a lavish private train, built in England in 1842 especially for Queen Victoria.

The **Golden Eagle Trans-Siberian Express** travels 10,000km (6,000 miles) from Moscow to the Russian Far East – one of the longest train journeys in the world.

16831

686

PALACE ON WHEELS

PALACE ON WHEELS

Inside the train is a lounge, a bar, two restaurants, a spa and a library.

This is the **Pride of Africa's** observation coach, where passengers admire the views through large windows at the end of the train.

During the 1920s and 1930s, the **Orient Express** was the most famous train in the world. Only wealthy people could afford to travel in this glamorous 'moving hotel'.

Inside this sleeper coach, passengers are provided with comfortable beds to sleep in overnight.

Royal crest

On board the **Palace on Wheels**, passengers are served drinks by personal attendants. Each coach is beautifully decorated in red and gold.

High-speed trains

The fastest trains today are powered by electricity. They travel on separate tracks from other trains.

This Japanese high-speed train is called a **bullet train**, because it has a smooth, rounded front, like a bullet.

This **tilting train** is designed to tip slightly as it goes around a bend. This way it can keep up a high speed without flinging passengers from side to side.

These rams lift the coach to one side as it goes around the bend, but the passengers can't feel it.

This train can travel at speeds of up to 250km/h (155mph).

Most bullet trains can fit over 1,300 passengers inside.

Bullet trains can travel at 300km/h (186mph).

This **Maglev** train hovers over a special track using strong magnets, instead of wheels.

Driver's cab

These metal coils are magnets powered by electricity. They push against magnets underneath the train to raise it up and make it move.

Maglev tracks are called guideways.

Biggest, longest, fastest...

The BIGGEST DIESEL LOCOMOTIVE ever built was the **Union Pacific 6922**. It was around three times heavier than many modern passenger locomotives.

The locomotive was 30m (98ft) long – that's almost three times longer than a double-decker bus.

This **J-R Maglev** is the FASTEST TRAIN in the world. It has reached a top speed of 581km/h (361mph).

The LONGEST ever train was the **BHP Iron Ore train**. It was made up of 682 wagons, pulled by eight diesel locomotives.

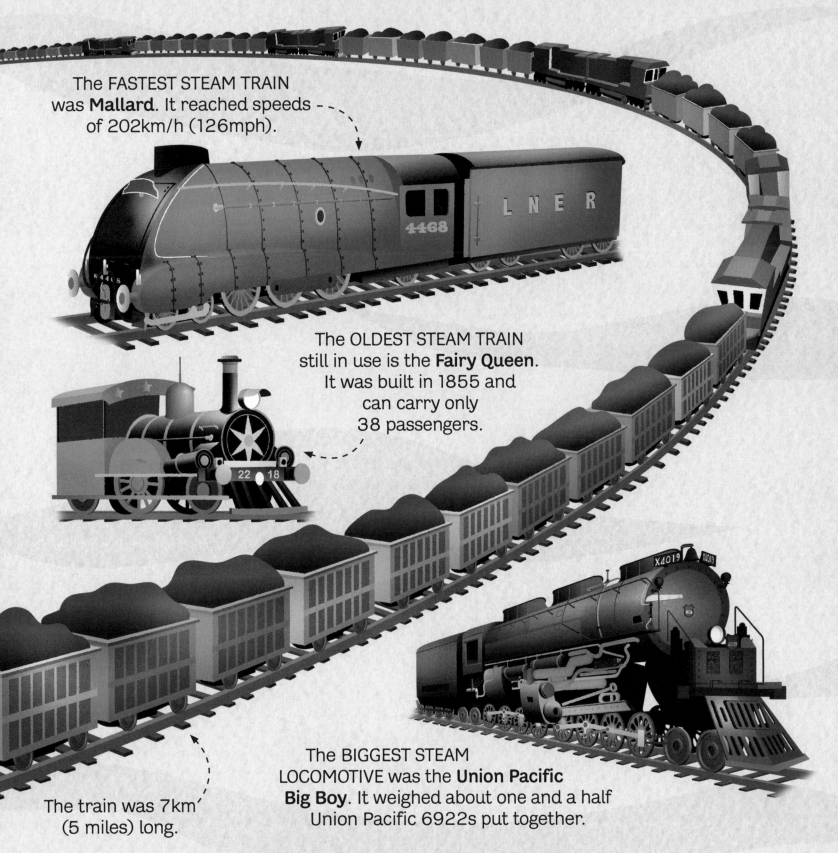

The FASTEST STEAM TRAIN
was **Mallard**. It reached speeds
of 202km/h (126mph).

The OLDEST STEAM TRAIN
still in use is the **Fairy Queen**.
It was built in 1855 and
can carry only
38 passengers.

The BIGGEST STEAM
LOCOMOTIVE was the **Union Pacific
Big Boy**. It weighed about one and a half
Union Pacific 6922s put together.

The train was 7km
(5 miles) long.

Series editors: Jane Chisholm and Alex Frith
Additional design: Laura Wood and Will Dawes   Digital design: John Russell

This edition first published in 2018 by Usborne Publishing Ltd., Usborne House, 83-85 Saffron Hill, London EC1N 8RT, England.
www.usborne.com Copyright © 2018, 2013 Usborne Publishing Ltd.